Awakening Your Chakras

A Magical Journey of Transformation Through Your Chakras

Jaya Sarada
& Arielle Beauduy

Disclaimer and Copyright Notice

Medical Disclaimer

IMPORTANT: This book is not intended to substitute for the advice of physicians or other health care providers. It provides information to help readers collaborate with health professionals to achieve optimal health. All rights reserved. Neither this book nor any part may be reproduced or transmitted in any form or by any means, electronic or mechanical, including photocopying, microfilming and recording, or by any information storage and retrieval system, without permission in writing from the publisher.

Medical Disclaimer

This book is designed to help readers collaborate with their physicians and other healthcare providers. It is not intended to replace professional medical advice, diagnosis, or treatment. Readers are encouraged to consult qualified health professionals regarding any medical conditions or concerns. The information presented here is intended to supplement, not replace, the expertise and recommendations of medical practitioners.

Contact Information

Divine Light Publishing
P.O. Box 1110
Gleneden Beach, Oregon 97388
Phone: 1.855-505.3935
Email: jaya@divinelightpublishing.com
For inquiries, please contact Divine Light Publishing at
1-800-505-3935 or via email at jaya@divinelightpublishing.com.

Our Soul's Journey

The Journey of Self-Discovery

A disciple approached Jesus and asked, *"Speak to us about our end: How will it look? How will it happen?"* Jesus responded, *"Have you found the beginning in yourselves? If not, why are you asking about the end? For in the place in yourselves where you find the beginning, you will also find the end. The Blessed ones will find their feet standing at the beginning. They will know the end and will not taste death."*
– Gospel of Thomas

The Gift of the Physical Body

As you journey through life, you are destined to remember your true nature. The physical body serves as a vehicle for this journey. In your outer life, you will experience a multitude of stories, relationships, and changes. Along the way, moments of pain and suffering may arise, as well as times of peace and happiness. Yet beneath these shifting experiences lies a more profound wisdom waiting to be discovered—a wisdom that quietly observes and guides you from within. By turning inward, you begin to recognize that this silent witness has always been present, offering insight and clarity as you move through the unfolding chapters of your life, inviting you to connect with the fullness of your existence and the secret wisdom life holds.

The Secret Wisdom of Life

Life holds a secret available to you—a wisdom that encompasses the fullness of your existence. As you reflect on your childhood and the experiences that shaped you, you may recognize that something has always been observing your life. This witness has continued through adulthood, sometimes offering guidance and insight along your path. This quiet presence, often unnoticed yet ever present, becomes more apparent when you pause to look within. It is not bound by the stories or events of your life; rather, it observes with gentle wisdom, inviting you to see beyond the surface as you turn your attention toward this inner witness, a sense of connection and clarity emerges, guiding you to understand the deeper patterns and meaning woven throughout your journey. By acknowledging and embracing this awareness, you open yourself to the transformative power of self-discovery, where each moment offers an opportunity to awaken to your true nature and expand into the fullness of your being.

Discovering the Witness Within

Who is this witness?

When you look deeply, you discover that this witness is your own true consciousness—pure awareness itself. When you turn your attention toward this awareness, you realize you are on an eternal journey of expansion, moving beyond the fleeting expressions of this present life.

As you rest in this awareness, life's ever-changing experiences appear as passing clouds drifting across the vast sky of your being, each moment offering an opportunity to witness rather than identify with the drama or story unfolding. In this spacious presence, you begin to sense the innate peace and freedom that arise from simply being, untouched by the circumstances of the world. The more you return to this quiet center, the more you realize that roles, achievements, or challenges do not define your essence—it is the silent, luminous field from which all experience arises and to which it returns. By honoring this inner witness, you open yourself to deeper clarity, acceptance, and a profound sense of belonging that infuses every aspect of your journey.

CONTENTS

Introduction

The Seven Chakras are the *Jewels of Light* located along the spinal cord. It is important to keep them clear and balanced, allowing a free flow of energy through the spine so that your Spirit is free to express the radiant being that you are, unencumbered by accumulated or unresolved issues.

Balancing the chakras can be accomplished through guided meditations, yoga and movement, energy healing methods and connecting with nature. When your chakras are balanced you will have a greater vitality and increased sense of joy and well-being. Since the chakras are deeply interconnected with energy fields and our connection to Spirit, by keeping them balanced you will achieve vibrant well-being.

This book will provide you with information on the seven major chakras as well as the three higher chakras. In this book you'll find many ways to connect with your chakras and your energy. You can use any or all of the methods here to help keep your chakras balanced and assist in transforming your life so you may live to your fullest potential. Listen to your body and intuition and enjoy this magical journey of transformation through your chakras.

"Wisdom is knowing I am nothing,
Love is knowing I am everything,
and between the two my life moves."
– Nisargadatta Maharaj

The Seven Jewels of Magical Transformation

When we look closely at the wonders of nature, we begin to recognize magic in every aspect of life. This magic is the very force that gives vitality to all of nature, and, in essence, it is what we are made of as well. By understanding this, we see that nature's vitality and creativity are reflected within us, forming a deep connection between ourselves and the world around us.

Awakening Your Chakras serves as a path to discover and embody your best self. Through this journey, you are guided to reach for your highest potential, aligning your inner nature with the magical energy that animates all of existence.

The 1st Jewel of Awakening: Root Chakra

The first jewel emerges from your Ground of Being and is closely associated with the **Root Chakra**. When the Root Chakra is awakened, you feel a deep sense of unity with life and the natural world. This is the foundation for your journey of transformation, where you affirm your sacred contract and wholeheartedly say "Yes" to your life purpose. It all begins at this grounding level, setting the stage for the unfolding of your highest potential.

The 2nd Jewel of Awakening: Navel Chakra

The second jewel is the gift of Energy and Confidence, residing in the **Navel Chakra**. Within this center, the creative energy that exists within you mirrors the same force that brings forth the wonders of nature. When you access this jewel, confidence and creativity flow more freely, serving as a channel for the life force and pure potential that reside in every being.

The 3rd Jewel of Awakening: Solar Plexus Chakra

The third jewel is found in Courage and Strength and is connected to the **Solar Plexus Chakra**. As you progress on your journey of awakening, you move beyond old patterns and limited ideas of yourself. This stage calls for true courage and inner strength, empowering you to make choices that are aligned with the Divine and your highest self.

The 4th Jewel of Awakening: Heart Chakra

The fourth jewel is discovered in the depths of your **Heart Chakra**, which is like a Sacred Chalice of Divine Love. By nurturing compassion, love, forgiveness, and a sense of unity, your heart opens to greater measures of divine light and consciousness.

The 5th Jewel of Awakening: Throat Chakra

The fifth jewel is the center for Truth and Miracles, residing in the Throat Chakra, which is linked to your willpower. When your will aligns with your highest intention and potential, you naturally reach for the greater good and strengthen your connection to your sacred source. This alignment places responsibility for your soul's growth on you, leading you to make choices that support your well-being and spiritual evolution.

The 6th Jewel of Awakening: Third Eye Chakra

The sixth jewel is Harmony and Clarity, corresponding to the **Third Eye Chakra**. At this level, your inner self awakens, enabling you to perceive truth in direct communion with the Divine Source. The activation of this jewel brings universal principles of truth to life within you, illuminating your path with clarity, discernment, and a sense of divine order and beauty.

The 7th Jewel of Awakening: Crown Chakra

The seventh jewel is a diamond frequency of Integration and Unity Consciousness, associated with the **Crown Chakra**. Through the ongoing evolution of your soul, you come to understand yourself as an expression of the Divine Source. The **Crown Chakra** becomes a channel for Divine Guidance, serving as a bridge between your physical self and higher consciousness. At this level, innocence, purity, sparkling joy, and a profound love of life are revealed.

In this present moment, you are whole, free, and connected to the magic within. It is a space of peace and joy—a true sense of belonging and home. Deep within, each person holds a treasure chest of wonder, light, joy, innocence, and hope. This inner sanctuary is the wellspring of divine power, wisdom, guidance, and profound peace. It remains untouched by negative beliefs or fears, protected always by the laws of divine love.

Enjoy your Magical Journey!

At any moment, you have a choice, that either leads you closer to your spirit or further away from it.

Thich Nhat Hanh

The Wish-Fulfilling Tree

The Divine Nature of the Wish-Fulfilling Tree

The Wish-Fulfilling Tree is a powerful metaphor for the nature of God. Just as the tree grants wishes to those who sit beneath its branches, God responds to the thoughts and beliefs of those in His presence. If a person approaches God with a sense of lack or poverty, that feeling persists. However, those who believe with conviction that God will fulfill their desires receive blessings accordingly. God's kindness is such that He provides for His devotees even before they ask, knowing their thoughts and intentions. When wishes are made with pure faith, they are surely fulfilled.

As one rests beneath the shade of the Wish-Fulfilling Tree, a sense of tranquility and trust begins to blossom, nurturing the soul's hope and anticipation for divine grace. In this sacred space, the individual is reminded that the heart's intentions and the clarity of one's faith draw forth the benevolence of the universe, much like the gentle unfolding of leaves in sunlight. This mystical interaction teaches that surrendering doubts and embracing unwavering trust not only aligns us with God's boundless generosity but also opens the way for miracles to manifest in everyday life quietly. With each sincere, faith-filled wish, the connection to the Divine deepens, and one learns that the true power of the Wish-Fulfilling Tree lies within the harmony of belief, gratitude, and the peaceful assurance that blessings are ever-present for those who receive with an open heart.

The Power of Faith and Positive Affirmation

It is essential to maintain unwavering faith in God and to nurture positive affirmations in the mind. Every thought and every word is an affirmation, shaping our reality. By cultivating positive thoughts, we invite the blessings of the Wish-Fulfilling Tree, allowing God to fill our lives with goodness. Conversely, harboring negativity brings about adverse outcomes. One must be vigilant not to let negativity, symbolized as the tiger, consume them. Instead, let positivity guide your mind and your life, ensuring that the benevolence of the Wish-Fulfilling Tree is always present.

As faith and affirmation work together to attract blessings, so too does gratitude deepen our connection with the divine source of all abundance. By consciously appreciating the gifts present in each moment, we heighten our receptivity to life's goodness and expand the presence of peace within our hearts. This open-hearted gratitude not only draws more positivity into our experience but also strengthens our energy field, allowing us to remain grounded and resilient amidst life's challenges. In this way, our thoughts, words, and attitudes shape an energetic foundation that supports spiritual growth and invites the universe's benevolence to flow freely into every aspect of our lives.

The Aura & Energy Fields

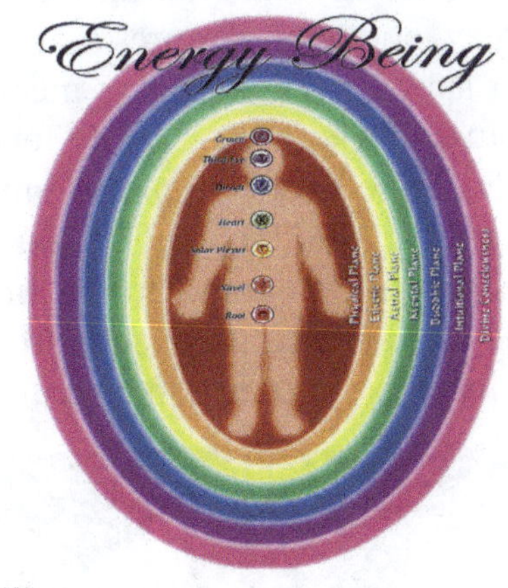

Understanding the Aura

The word "Aura" is derived from the Greek term Aura, meaning breeze. Humans are multidimensional beings surrounded by spiraling energy spheres that radiate outward from the physical body, creating luminous energy fields. The journey of self-discovery begins with the physical body, serving as the foundational layer for experiencing and understanding these energy fields. As we delve deeper into the nature of the aura, we recognize that these energetic layers not only reflect our physical health but also mirror our emotions and thoughts, subtly interacting with the spiritual essence within. The aura acts as both a shield and a transmitter, responding to our inner vibrational states and connecting us to the broader tapestry of existence. Through conscious awareness and practices of gratitude and mindfulness, our energy fields become more vibrant and receptive, allowing us to sense the divine presence and experience greater harmony within ourselves. This expanded perception reveals that our journey of self-discovery is enriched by understanding these energy fields, which serve as bridges between the physical world and the eternal soul, guiding us toward more profound spiritual realization and a life filled with radiant well-being.

As our awareness of the aura deepens, we come to appreciate how each layer—from the etheric to the emotional—contributes to the dynamic flow of energy that defines our overall vitality. This intricate interplay not only nurtures our physical and emotional health but also subtly influences our mental clarity and spiritual growth. By attuning to these subtle energies and embracing practices that foster self-reflection and inner balance, we build a foundation for lasting well-being. This journey invites us to honor the interconnectedness of body, mind, and spirit, allowing the luminous fields surrounding us to support our transformation and guide us ever closer to our truest, most radiant self.

The Divine Union of Body and Soul

The physical body serves as a vessel for the realization of the divine and eternal soul within each individual. Through this vehicle, the inner being can explore the full spectrum of human experience, expressing the divine essence that resides at our core. When we allow our spirit, or divine nature, to reveal itself in our daily lives, we witness the unfolding of a profound miracle—one that bridges our human existence with the sacred. Remembering our true and unchanging identity enables us to transcend fleeting narratives and reconnect with our deeper nature. By deepening our awareness of the sacred union of body and soul, every moment becomes an opportunity to embody our highest self and illuminate the world with the light of spirit. Honoring the physical vessel while nurturing the soul's journey helps us attune to the subtle energies that surround and flow through us—energies that mirror our emotions, thoughts, and spiritual intentions. This harmonious relationship calls us to live authentically, fostering creativity and love in our interactions. As we move from a sense of separation toward unity with the divine source, embracing the miracle of our true nature empowers us to radiate well-being and spiritual vitality, supporting our ongoing path to self-realization and vibrant wholeness.

The Soul's Radiant Presence and Energy Fields

Awareness of the soul's luminous presence awakens us to the subtle interplay between our spiritual core and the surrounding aura and energy fields. This sacred recognition invites us to honor each layer of our being—the physical, emotional, mental, and spiritual—as facets of an interconnected tapestry woven with divine intention. By embracing the gentle shifts and resonant energies that flow through us, we cultivate inner harmony, which in turn supports our journey toward spiritual fulfillment. The soul's eternal light serves as a guiding force, illuminating the path to deeper wisdom and authentic self-expression. When we enter a state of grace, we become receptive to the universe's blessings, finding meaning and connection in every experience. Through mindful presence and heartfelt gratitude, our energy fields are revitalized, allowing the vitality of spirit to infuse our everyday lives. This inspiration moves us to live with clarity, compassion, and joy, perpetually guided by the radiant force of the soul within.

You have to grow from the inside out. None can teach you, none can make you spiritual. There is no other teacher but your own soul.

Swami Vivekananda

Your Energy Fields

The Etheric Field

The Etheric Field serves as the blueprint of the physical body. It is the first energy band, forming a luminous layer that surrounds and protects the body from external influences. Often referred to as the health aura, the Etheric Field reflects the individual's vitality; its strength and radiance are direct indicators of well-being. The colors and brightness of the aura reveal the condition of the Etheric Field, showing whether the streams of vital force flowing within are strong or weak. Just beyond the Etheric Field lies the emotional layer of the aura, a dynamic realm intimately connected to our feelings and vitality. As the quality of our thoughts and intentions influences the emotional field, nurturing it with positivity and healing affirmations allows it to radiate joy and well-being throughout our being. When the emotional field is clear and vibrant, it enhances both our physical and energetic health, supporting a harmonious and resilient state of being. By fostering mindful awareness and tending to the subtle energies within and around us, we not only strengthen our protective layers but also cultivate a deeper sense of peace and spiritual fulfillment in everyday life.

The Emotional Body

The emotional field is the next layer of the aura and serves as the source of our feelings and vitality. When negative thinking contaminates this field, it leads to unhappiness and emotional unrest. By nurturing the emotional field with positive thoughts, intentions, and healing affirmations, it begins to radiate joy and vibrant wellness, positively influencing our overall state of being. As we deepen our understanding of the emotional field's influence on our well-being, it becomes clear that cultivating mindful presence is essential to fostering clarity and inner peace. Rather than letting unresolved emotions or anxious thoughts dominate our experience, we can practice attentive awareness in the present moment, supporting emotional equilibrium and nurturing a harmonious connection with ourselves. This conscious approach empowers us to transform

Vibrant Well-Being Through Chakra Transformation

The Chakras hold the key to our well-being, opening doorways to our full potential. Each chakra serves as a gateway to transformation, and when transcended, they enable a steady stream of well-being throughout our lives.

Root Chakra

At the foundation lies the Root Chakra, often associated with fear and insecurity. Transformation occurs when these feelings are addressed through affirmations centered on trust, gratitude, and a sincere intention to serve. Through this process, fear is transcended, fostering a sense of safety and grounding.

Navel Chakra

The Navel Chakra is closely linked to guilt, blocked creativity, and abandonment. By focusing on self-acceptance, embracing creativity, and cultivating self-love, these challenges can be transcended. This process opens the door to authentic expression and strengthens a positive relationship with oneself.

emotional patterns and embrace each day with renewed strength and serenity, laying the foundation for vibrant well-being and spiritual growth.

The Mental Body

The Field of the Mental Body is the next layer of the aura, intimately connected to the realm of thought, focus, and intention. This energetic layer shapes how we perceive and respond to our experiences, influencing our ability to maintain clarity, presence, and emotional equilibrium. When our thoughts are harmonious and directed with mindful intent, the mental field radiates with light and stability, supporting the emotional and physical layers beneath. By cultivating positive thinking and conscious awareness, we invite transformative clarity into our lives, creating space for deeper healing and a vibrant sense of well-being. This process of nurturing the mental body aligns seamlessly with the journey of presence and clarity, allowing us to dissolve distractions, restore balance, and open ourselves to spiritual insight and authentic connection with our highest self.

The Spiritual Body

The Field of the Spiritual Body forms the outermost layer of the aura, encompassing and uplifting all the energy fields beneath it. This luminous field connects the individual to universal consciousness and the divine source, serving as a bridge between material existence and spiritual truth. When the spiritual body is harmonized, it infuses every aspect of our being with grace, wisdom, and clarity, supporting the journey toward self-realization and unity. By nurturing this field through mindfulness, devotion, and inner alignment, we invite spiritual insight and a deeper sense of purpose into our daily lives. As the surrounding energies—emotional, mental, and physical—find balance, the spiritual body radiates a profound sense of peace and clarity, guiding us into the transformative power of presence and the spiritual growth reflected in the chapters ahead.

Solar Plexus Chakra

The Solar Plexus Chakra is associated with shame and a lack of self-confidence. Transformation here involves surrendering these feelings and embracing self-confidence, aligning personal will with a higher source. This empowers individuals to act with integrity and purpose.

Heart Chakra

Sadness and sorrow reside in the Heart Chakra. Through intentional inner work that involves releasing the past, these emotions are transcended. This allows unconditional love, compassion, and joy to emerge, benefiting both oneself and others.

Throat Chakra

The Throat Chakra often reflects the suppression of truth and unexpressed potential. Transformation is achieved by fostering empowerment through thought, practicing truthful speech, and cultivating the ability to listen deeply. This enables authentic self-expression and communication.

Third Eye Chakra

Uncertainty and misunderstandings are common challenges within the Third Eye Chakra. These are transcended by cultivating clear seeing, intuition, and peaceful understanding, which support insight and a deeper connection to inner wisdom.

Crown Chakra

The Crown Chakra may be affected by confusion and a lack of direction. Integration, unity, and profound guidance from Spirit are realized as these limitations are transcended, supporting a harmonious connection with the spiritual dimension

Our Core Light Channel- The Flow of Life Force

Flowing through each chakra, our Core Light Channel serves as the conduit for vital energy, weaving together the transformative qualities of self-confidence, compassion, authentic expression, intuition, and spiritual unity. As we consciously open and align this channel, the life force flows freely, supporting our growth and illuminating our path. In this dynamic movement, we experience the seamless integration of body, mind, and spirit, allowing our inner radiance to shine and guide us on our journey rooted in our being.

As the Core Light Channel flows unhindered, it harmonizes our energetic centers and fosters a profound sense of alignment with our highest intentions. This vibrant connection not only nurtures our inner light but also amplifies our capacity for clarity, wisdom, and loving presence. Through this ongoing dance of energy, we become receptive to subtle spiritual guidance and empowered to walk our path with confidence and grace. The illuminating force within us enhances every aspect of our existence, infusing each moment with purpose and awareness and inviting us to cultivate a deeper connection with the divine essence that resides at the heart of all life.

Let the breath lead the way.
                    Sharon Salzberg

Kundalini - Life Force Energy

Kundalini is the rising or awakening of our life force from its latent state. The root word, Kundal, means to coil, depicting a snake-like energy which lies dormant at the base of the spine in the root chakra. When Kundalini begins to awaken, its purifying fire clears our core light channel or Sushumna Channel. Kundalini is stimulated through all forms of yoga, meditation, energy medicine techniques, the creative arts and nature.

Shiva and Shakti - Unity of Duality

Shakti depicts our creative life force or prana and the ever changing energy of matter. Shiva depicts our unchanging, unlimited, infinite pure consciousness. Shiva and Shakti are ultimately two different sides of the same coin, the all-one divine consciousness. When Kundalini Shakti, the rising creative force, is awakened it begins to travel up the Sushumuna channel, located along the spinal column. It is the desire of Shakti, the energy of Creation, to be reunited with Shiva, the energy of Spirit. This longing becomes the catalyst for the transcendence of the lower chakras. As Shakti travels upward, it disentangles the knots of each chakra which allows them to blossom. When each chakra opens it imparts aspects of our selves that are calling for transformation. A tremendous cosmic unity is experienced when Kundalini Shakti merges with its counter, Shiva. This awakening of true love and wisdom is fully realized in the Crown Chakra and then lays to rest in the temple of the heart. With all chakras open and fully energized the journey is complete and all our experiences are integrated transcending time, space and form.

The Seven Chakras - Your Inner Jewels

The chakras (meaning wheels of light) are whirling centers of vital energy. Each is shaped like a vertical cone. The chakras are seeded in the Sushumna Channel. Chakras function as storage centers   they energize, control and are responsible for proper functioning of our body, mind and emotions. Our life energy flows in an interweaving channel from the Root Chakra up the spine to the Crown Chakra and where it crosses it forms a chakra. These energy centers give the appearance of a brilliant lotus with unfolding petals. When the chakras are blended and integrated they are instruments of divine power and glory. In a state of illumination the chakras are like jewels strung upon the necklace of the Sushumna Channel.

There are seven major chakras   four in the body, and three in the head. There are also many minor chakras throughout the body, as well as the higher spiritual chakras above the head and the mother earth chakra below the feet.

The seven major chakras have a close correspondence to the endocrine glands and are related to the major organs. They play an important part in nourishing and sustaining the nervous system, organs and glands. The chakras also have a direct relationship to our emotions and our belief system, offering us keys to our evolution as spiritual beings. The chakras function as communicators or transmitters of energy from one energy field to another, working in unison to provide the most optimal condition for awakening. The first three chakras – Root, Navel and Solar Plexus – are related to earth, water and fire. The Heart Chakra is related to the element air, the Throat Chakra to light and the Third Eye and Crown Chakras are related to the integration of all elements, making up the spiritual and divine aspect of our being. related to the integration of all elements, making up the spiritual and divine aspect of our being.

The spiritual journey is the unlearning of fear and the acceptance of love.

Marianne Williamson

1ˢᵗ Jewel

Root Chakra

Our Ground of Being

The first chakra, Muladhara, meaning "SUPPORT AT THE ROOT," is the keeper of our beginnings in this world and the bearer of our foundation. It is located at the base of the spine. This chakra is a whirling vortex of energy flowing into the reproductive organs. It energizes the sexual organs and externalizes as adrenal glands, governing the spine and kidneys. Kundalini, the serpent fire, resides here. The Root Chakra is related to the physical and etheric field subtle bodies, with the element of Earth and the sense of smell.

The Root Chakra provides us with keys to our life purpose. In the Root center we hold the information about our family of origin and ancestral memories. The home of our basic instincts, the Root Chakra drives us to find sexual unity, passion and the fire of life. This fire gives stability, power and the instinct to survive. Our Root deepens our relationship with joy and gratitude for being alive.

In order to maintain balance, the Root Chakra must be in harmony with the Third Eye and Crown Chakras. When we work with the higher centers in our transformation process we create a new sense of grounding. Integration of our lower three chakras with the chakras of our soul, reconnects us with our divine purpose in life. The Crown center brings a security that is everlasting as it connects us with the divine creator of life. The Third Eye center brings our clear vision and connects us with the wisdom to tell the real from the unreal.

Yoga Postures: Bridge Pose, Full Locust, Head to Knee Pose

When this center is balanced, one has developed a deep trust in life. They honor life with gratitude and understand life's changing ebb and flow. Their life energy is intact and they have a reverence for Mother Nature.

Within you there is a stillness and a sanctuary to which you can retreat at any time and be yourself.

Hermann Hesse

Navel Chakra

Energy & Confidence

The second chakra, Svadhistana, meaning "DWELLING IN THE PLACE OF SWEETNESS," is known for where the sea of our emotions reside. It is located at the midpoint of the sacrum. This chakra externalizes as the reproductive glands and governs the reproductive system. The Navel Chakra is related to the etheric field subtle body, and the element of Water with the sense of hearing.

The life force circulates from this chakra with the purpose of nurturing the physical creative force. Energy comes into the field through the spleen and then is distributed to the remaining chakras.

When in balance, the Navel Chakra creates a sense of abundance and appreciation for what life brings. This chakra is considered the seat of Shakti, where our physical, sexual and creative energy is expressed. It is the place of life, conception, change and movement. It can be visualized as a bright sphere of radiant orange light bringing forth creative energies and ideas. This chakra holds the magical wonder of our being and is related to the ages of eight to fourteen, when we most experience life's sweetness and unconditional joy.

The Navel Chakra represents change, duality, movement, flexibility and creative flow. When we energetically tune into this center we can observe that life is best served when we allow ourself to experience it in an unconditional manner.

The energy of the Navel Chakra works closely with the Ajna, or Third Eye Chakra.

Yoga Postures: Leg Lifts, Triangle, Cobra, Spinal Twist

When this chakra is balanced, there are harmonious and connected feelings in one's life. One has healthy sexual feelings, creative expression, and is considerate and friendly with others. One exudes healthiness and vibrancy, has a good self-esteem and positive relationships.

Realize deeply that the present moment is all you have. Make the now the primary focus of your life.

Eckhart Tolle

Solar Plexus Chakra

Courage & Strength

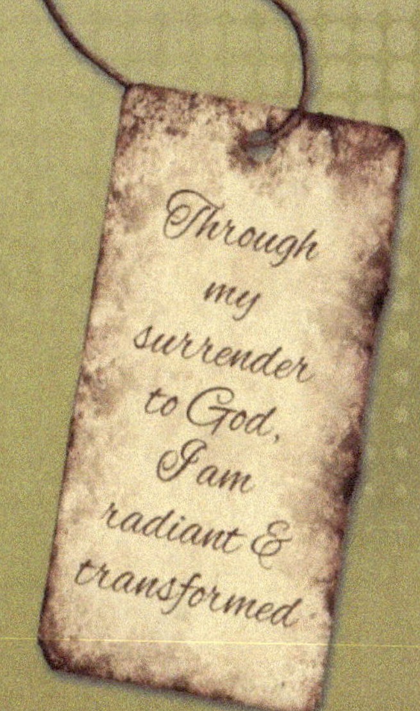

The third chakra, Manipura, meaning "CITY OF JEWELS," is known for being our power center. It is located between our navel and sternum. The Solar Plexus Chakra receives and distributes energy throughout the physical form. This chakra corresponds to the liver, kidneys and large intestine. The Solar Plexus Chakra is related to the astral and emotional field subtle bodies, with the element of Fire and the sense of sight. Because Manipura is the power center of the physical field, where instincts and survival play an important role, it is easily exhausted. Modern society works through the Solar Plexus Chakra. People are conditioned to fulfill desires, seek personal power and build a false sense of self. The Solar Plexus is our guide to the world around us and provides us with an important protective force until our inner light becomes completely balanced.

The energy of the Solar Plexus Chakra is linked deeply with the heart. The goal of this chakra is to transcend our personal self, and allow ourselves to connect with the inherent unity in life and the true wisdom that comes with this knowing. As we let go of our personal striving, the lotus of the Solar Plexus turns from pointing downward to pointing upward to the heart, forming a bridge of light that assists the lower chakras to unite with the higher.

A journey into our Heart Chakra is an experience of peace and calmness.

Yoga Postures: Bow, The Boat, Sun Salutation

When this center is balanced, there is a feeling of peace and harmony with one's inner self. Actions are performed with a deep reverence for life; light and energy are expressed. Wishes can magically fulfill spontaneously because of the emission of light that the individual gives.

Being at ease with not knowing is crucial for answers to come to you.

Eckhart Tolle

Heart Chakra

Sacred Chalice of Infinite Love

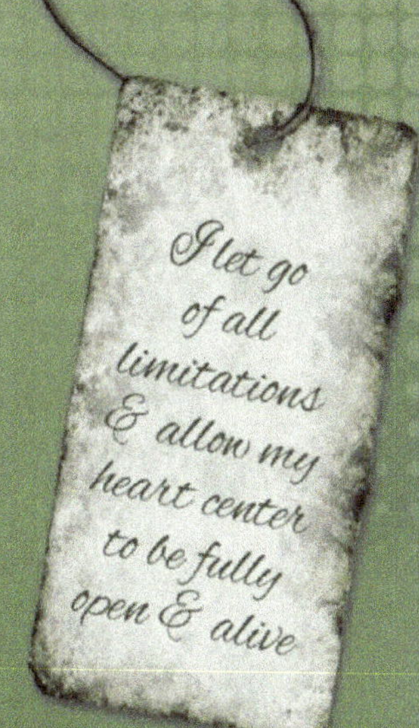

The fourth chakra, Anahara, meaning "UNSTRUCK," is the source of all light and love. It is located in the center of the chest and is where the lower chakras and the higher chakras meet and become integrated, creating oneness of being. The Heart Chakra is related to the mental field subtle body, and the element of Air with the sense of touch. The Heart Chakra is a bridge of light between the lower centers and the higher. All must cross this bridge to move from the limited consciousness of personality to divine consciousness.

The Heart center opening demonstrates the deepest action of love turned inward. The Heart Chakra functions to protect, heal and bring balance to the body, mind and emotions. Because this chakra is closely associated with the thymus gland, which governs the immune system, it is quite vulnerable to our overall level of health. The Heart Chakra awakens us to the qualities of love, forgiveness and compassion helping to release the painful memories of the past. The forgiveness process opens the door to true compassion for our life and our relationships and creates the miracle of understanding. The Heart Chakra opens when the personal will is transformed to divine will and personal power evolves to an empowered heart devoted to peace, giving and receiving love and the practice of discernment. Unconditional love, compassion towards others and ourselves replaces self-centered desire and want. Cherishing our sacred energy, we give from our overflowing heart.

When our heart and spirit are integrated we manifest a life of beauty and joy. Our Heart center is our emotional center where we transform our life through Divine Love. Breathing deeply, allow this Divine Love to open your heart and heal your life!

Yoga Postures: Cobra, Fish, Full Bridge, Camel, Sun Salutation

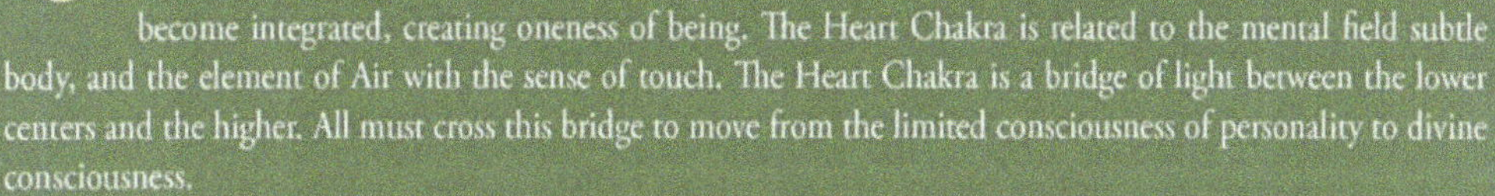

*When this center is balanced, all centers are in harmony.
There is a feeling of unconditional love and surrender to a higher will.
There is a radiance of love, sincerity, compassion and a deep feeling of wholeness.*

The spiritual journey is the unlearning of fear and the acceptance of love.

Marianne Williamson

5th Jewel

Throat Chakra

Truth & Miracles

The fifth chakra, Visuddha, meaning "PURE PLACE," is the chakra of purification and miracles. It is located at the base of the neck. The Throat Chakra governs the vocal chords, bronchia, lungs and digestive tract and externalizes as the thyroid and parathyroid glands, which metabolize the energy of the system. The Throat Chakra is related to the buddhic subtle body, with the element of Ether and the sense of hearing. It is called the chakra of miracles for its connection with the powers of life and its ability to express clear intentions through the spoken word.

The journey of consciousness takes us through the limitations of the lower chakras into the higher centers of our true self. In the realm of the Throat Chakra, Visuddha, we have the opportunity to express the joy of pure beingness through the voice. The Throat center teaches us to use sound, prayer and affirmations for healing and balancing any discord of our body, mind and emotions. The highest expression of the Throat Chakra is prayer, when one communes with their true self and God. Prayer develops a deep devotion and surrender to the highest will of the divine.

The Throat Chakra is the primary center of healing and transformation of ourselves. When this center is balanced, we express the truth of our authentic self which creates an opening for the grace of healing to take place.

Yoga Postures: Neck Rolls, Fish Pose, Shoulder Stand, The Plough

*When this chakra is balanced, an individual expresses thoughts, feelings and emotions without fear.
One is honest with themselves and others.
Speech is clear, reflecting inner truth. Silence is easily practiced.*

Within you there is a stillness and a sanctuary to which you can retreat at any time and be yourself.

Hermann Hesse

6th Jewel

Third Eye Chakra

Harmony & Clarity

The sixth chakra, Ajna, meaning "COMMAND," is the center of higher intuition. It is located between the eyebrows on the forehead. The Third Eye Chakra is related to the intuitive field subtle body, with the element of Ether and our sixth sense of inner sight.

Our sixth sense, clairvoyance, is developed in the Third Eye Chakra. The related endocrine glands are the pineal and pituitary glands. It governs the eyes, teeth, sinuses, lower brain and the brain stem. When aligned with the soul it brings clear thinking and vision, intuition and truth. When balanced, this center gives the profound ability for one to manifest what they visualize in their life. When one opens this chakra, it merges the dual nature of life so it becomes unified and whole.

This is the master for all the other chakras. The opening of the Ajna is vitally important to achieving full potential in our lifetime. Quieting the mind, deep contemplation and inquiry into the nature of the true self are the paths to accomplishing this opening. This center, when fully awakened, has the power to transform all conditions of our life, which releases karmic patterns from the past and heals the body, mind and emotions. This chakra is awakened through meditation, where we become a vehicle to rest in the light of our pure consciousness.

Yoga Posture: Palming the Eyes, Meditation, Yoga Mudra, Fish

When this chakra is balanced, there is a developed level of perception and one is able to tune in to their inner voice.
One is able to attain the gift of visualization and the ability to comprehend life intuitively.

When the soul lies down in that grass, the world is too
full to talk about.

Rumi

7th Jewel
Crown Chakra
Diamond Frequency
Perception & Clarity

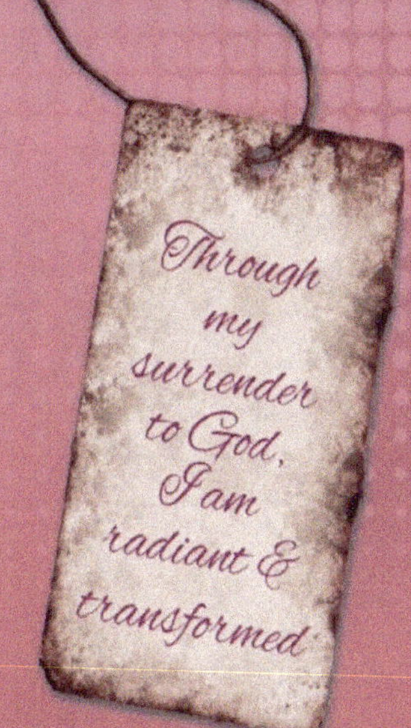

The seventh chakra, Sahashara, meaning "THOUSAND-PETALED LOTUS," is the chakra of unity. It is located on the crown of the head. It governs the brain and nervous system and externalizes as the pituitary and pineal gland. The Crown Chakra is related to the divine field subtle body, and the element of Cosmic Energy with the sense of thought. Through union and harmony of the Heart and Crown Chakras, love, will, and intelligence are balanced.

This exquisite white thousand-petaled lotus forms a beautiful crown on the head, with the Antahkarana or stem of the flower reaching upward toward the heavens. This stem is the bridge of light between our limited personality and our soul's divine energy. It is the soul's point of entry and exit into this human form and it is also the receiving and distributing station for our life force. The Crown Chakra is activated through our yearning to unite with our inner true nature.

Opening the Crown Chakra allows the divine to clear past impressions and to create an unconditional relationship to life based on the present. Jesus said, "Empty thyself and I shall fill thee," which implies a divine energy entering through the Crown. When we empty ourselves of the scars and conditioning of the past we are born anew into the light.

Yoga Postures: Half-lotus, Headstand, Meditation

When this center is balanced, one has transcended their belief that they are separate from God and has surrendered to the Divine presence within. They are in harmony with life and have acceptance of all that is.

In the silence of love, you will find the spark of life.

Rumi

Soul Meditation

Awakening as a Being of Light

You are a Being of Light, surrounded by a Halo of Divinity that offers Angelic protection. Within this halo, your higher chakras serve as gateways to your Divine Source and portals for Sacred Guidance. As you awaken to your true nature, the radiant light within you expands, illuminating each step of your spiritual journey. This vibrant energy flows through your core, aligning your chakras and inviting you to embody the wisdom and compassion of your Higher Self. With every breath, you deepen your connection to the Divine, effortlessly channeling guidance and inspiration. This sacred alignment nurtures your heart and mind, empowering you to move forward with clarity and grace, fully aware of your place within the loving web of creation.

Connecting to Guidance

To seek guidance, gently place your hand over your heart and focus on your higher chakras. When your heart and mind align with a single intention, you move closer to realizing your highest potential. As you connect with this inner guidance, allow each breath to deepen your sense of openness and expansion. Notice how the energy flows effortlessly from your heart upward, inviting clarity and a gentle release of any lingering tension. With every inhale, fill yourself with renewed vitality and purpose, and as you exhale, let go of doubt and welcome a profound peace within. This sacred practice nourishes your spirit, encouraging you to step forward with confidence, anchored in love and a clear sense of direction. Feel this harmonious integration ripple through your being, preparing you to embrace the next phase of your journey with trust and gratitude.

Breath and Expansion

Begin by taking slow, deep breaths. With every exhale, release any stress or worry. As you inhale, feel your sense of self and well-being expand, filling you with renewed energy. Allow each breath to carry you deeper into a place of openness, inviting a gentle sense of spaciousness throughout your body. Notice how, with every inhale, you awaken your inner light, and with each exhale, you let go of tension, making room for clarity and peace. This conscious breathing cultivates a state of calm and readiness, preparing you to channel divine energy and embrace the next phase of your spiritual journey with trust and gratitude.

Channeling Divine Energy

Direct your focus above your head and visualize a tube of light connecting Spirit to your Crown Chakra. Through this channel, divine energies pour in, bringing whispers of angelic guidance. Allow a deep peace to fill you as you ask for guidance, surrendering any resistance and trusting that your life unfolds for the highest good. Conclude your connection with Spirit by expressing deep gratitude, knowing, feeling, believing, and manifesting your request from the Universe. As you bask in this gentle awareness, feel the sacred energy flowing down through your channel of light, permeating your entire being with warmth and subtle vibrancy. Each breath you take integrates this divine essence, awakening your awareness of the interconnectedness of all creation and the blessing of divine alignment. Feel this luminous current harmonize your body, mind, and spirit, reinforcing your sense of belonging within the universal web. With this infusion of light, you are inspired to honor the infinite presence within and around you, stepping forward with openness and gratitude as you continue your journey of spiritual growth and conscious evolution.

Your Sacred Energy

Your Sacred Energy originates from the Source that animates all living things. This mysterious energy vibrates at different frequencies, forming the fabric of all creation. Life is woven into the web of Creation, blessed by the Divine Plan to evolve in Love and Consciousness.

We come to understand that everything is energy and that we are deeply interconnected. It becomes clear that we must care for our physical bodies as well as our thoughts and emotions. Our connection to the universal Spirit or God Light is the foundation of our joy. As we evolve, we increase our capacity to receive and express the Creator's Spiritual Light and Love.

Initiation of the Heart

Through heart initiation, balance and equanimity are achieved, freeing us from life's dualities. Sacred energy flows from the upper chakras into the lower chakras, infusing them with divine energy. The heart initiate is tested to release past attachments, such as lust, anger, greed, pride, and envy, attaining freedom from selfishness. By opening the heart center, we become spiritual warriors, protecting our sacred energy from illusion and cultivating harmlessness. The deer symbolizes the heart chakra, embodying ahimsa—the path of peace and complete trust in God. The opening of the heart can be a painful process, marking the transition from identifying with the temporary aspects of life. Cleansing emotional wounds and releasing the past allows the heart center to open. The luminous gateway of the heart leads to the antahkarana, the bridge of light enabling ascension to our true home. This sacred bridge is built on the complete release of spiritual ignorance and the sense of separateness. The heart chakra is the master station for the polarities within the emotional, mental, and etheric bodies, transforming lower impulses of personality chakras to reflect our divine essence.

I belong to no religion. My religion is love. Every heart is my temple.

Rumi

The Inner Sanctuary of the Heart

The Lotus Shrine Within

Deep within the castle of Brahman, which represents our physical body, lies a sacred, subtle shrine shaped like a lotus flower. Within this lotus lies a small, mysterious space, inviting us to turn inward and discover the true presence that dwells there. This is a call to seek understanding and connection with the indwelling essence, inviting a journey of inner exploration.

The Sanctuary of Silence

As we gently enter this quiet sanctuary, we begin to sense the boundless nature concealed within its simplicity. The lotus is not only a symbol but also a living space where the mysteries of existence are reflected in silence and light. Within this temple of the heart, the limitless horizon is revealed—the same infinite expanse found in the stars above and in the universe itself. Each mindful breath softens the boundary between self and cosmos, inviting recognition of the sacred unity at the core of all being. In this profound truth, we discover that the source of all creation dwells within our own hearts.

In this deep and tranquil space, the heart becomes both a sanctuary and a gateway, bridging the visible and the invisible realms. As silence settles, layers of illusion fall away, revealing the radiant presence that has always been within. Here, the boundaries between individual and universal consciousness dissolve, revealing a field of pure awareness and love.

Through mindful attention and reverent breathing, we learn to dwell in this sanctuary and listen to the quiet wisdom that arises from our innermost core. The journey inward is not a retreat from the world but a return to wholeness. In the heart's temple, we touch the eternal—the source of compassion, clarity, and strength. With each visit to this inner shrine, we deepen our understanding that the true self is inseparable from the vastness of creation. This realization brings peace, trust, and a lasting sense of belonging to the great web of life.

The Vastness Within the Heart

If one asks, "Who dwells in the small lotus-shaped shrine at the heart's center, within the castle of Brahman? Whom should we seek to know?" the answer reveals a profound truth. The small space within the heart is as vast as the infinite universe. Within this inner realm are the heavens, the earth, the sun, the moon, and the stars; fire, lightning, and winds; all that is, all that is not, and all possibilities. The entire universe is contained within this sacred presence, and He dwells within our heart.

Chandogya Upanishad

Guided Meditation: Entering the Lotus Shrine of the Heart

Settling Into Stillness

Close your eyes gently and settle your body into a comfortable position. Take a deep breath in, feeling your belly expand, then slowly release it, letting tension flow out of your body. With each inhale, imagine yourself drawing in gentle light, and with each exhale, let go of any distractions or worries.

Entering the Heart's Sanctuary

Bring your awareness to the center of your chest, to the quiet sanctuary of your heart. Visualize a beautiful lotus flower unfolding, its petals opening one by one. Within this lotus lies a luminous, peaceful space—a sacred inner shrine. Step softly inward and allow yourself to be welcomed by the stillness and light that dwell here.

Connecting to Inner Vastness

As you rest in this serene chamber, notice how the boundaries between yourself and the world begin to dissolve. Feel the   vastness within—an infinite horizon, as expansive as the stars above. Let each breath be a gentle bridge, connecting you to the divine presence at the core of your being.

Observing Thoughts with Compassion

If thoughts arise, observe them with compassion and let them drift away like clouds across the sky. Return to the quiet, radiant space within the lotus, where silence and wisdom reside. Feel the presence of love, awareness, and unity, knowing that the source of all creation dwells in your heart.

Returning with Peace and Gratitude

Stay here for a few moments, breathing in peace and breathing out gratitude. Allow any insights or feelings of wholeness to gently fill your being. When you are ready, return your awareness to your breath and your body, carrying with you the sense of connection and sacredness you have discovered within.

8th Jewel
Soul Star

White ~ Divine Guidance

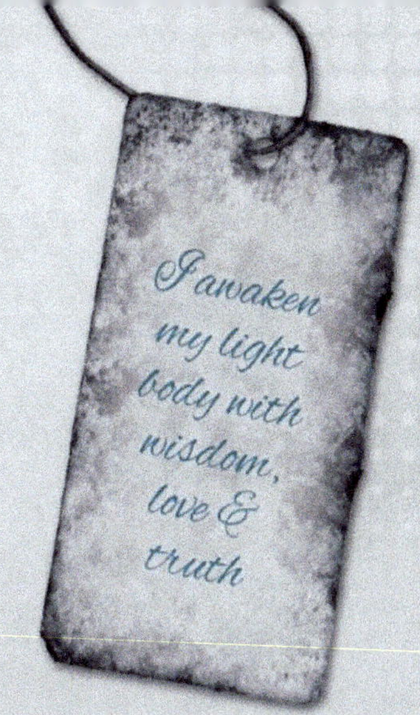

Color White for Soul Star • Silver for Earth Star
Gemstone- Stone White Selenite, Clear Quartz
Earth Star Grounding Stones -Smokey Quartz

The Soul Star Chakra is located about 4 to 5 inches above the head. This chakra is the center in which you receive universal inspiration and divine guidance. The Soul Star when harmonized expresses divine love, will and wisdom. This spiritual center holds infinite potential for enlightenment and transcendence. It is through deep surrender and letting go that we connect with our higher self and open this channel to receive divine guidance.

The Soul Star Chakra has its exact duplicate below the feet, known as the Earth Star Chakra – silver in color, and is known as the Terra Chakra. It provides the energy of deep grounding and connection to earth and it is a receptive energy, containing all the elements of earth, wind, fire and water.

Understanding our connection with our divine purpose in physical form and our spiritual awakening is an art that can be mastered through balancing and alignment of our entire chakra system. The Terra Chakra assists us in understanding our sacred earth contract and our unique life purpose while our Soul Star Chakra holds our potential as spiritual beings on a path of evolution.

Soul Star & Earth Star Meditation

Imagine yourself in a bubble of light that is surrounding you from the top of your head (your Soul Star) to below your feet (your Earth Star). Breathing deeply, visualize the light from the Soul Star traveling down through your head, through your body and deeply connecting with your Earth Star. As it travels, pay attention to any areas of your energy fields that could use support. Allow the light from your Soul Star to focus its healing energy where you may need attention. The light will do the work. Breathing out, let go of any constriction, pain or other resistance. Breathing in, allow the light to balance, harmonize, heal and bring peace to your life. Now focus your attention on the Earth Star Chakra, below your feet. Take a moment in deep prayer and send an affirmation of gratitude and affirm your life purpose as a being of light ready to offer service where needed.

The heart has its own language. The heart knows a hundred thousand
ways to speak.

Rumi

Opening Soul Star Meditation

Preparation and Grounding

Begin by finding a comfortable seat. Allow your body to settle, then place your hands gently on your lap. Take several slow, deep breaths, inviting calm and clarity into your being. As your awareness settles, bring your attention to the space just above the crown of your head.

Connecting to the Soul Star Chakra

Visualize a shimmering orb of pure white light hovering just above your head. This orb represents your Soul Star chakra—the gateway to spiritual wisdom and a sense of universal connection. With each inhale, imagine the orb expanding, its gentle energy cascading downward like starlight, enveloping your head and shoulders. On each exhale, feel this light merge with your energy, dissolving boundaries and opening you to receive higher guidance. Allow your consciousness to rise and meet the Soul Star, sensing the presence of your true self beyond daily concerns.

Affirmation and Presence

Silently affirm: "I am open to receiving light, love, and wisdom from my highest self." If thoughts or emotions arise, acknowledge them kindly and let them pass, returning your attention to the luminous star above. Rest in this spacious awareness, feeling your connection to all that is, and welcome any messages, visions, or feelings of peace that arise from this sacred space.

Integration and Closing

Stay in this meditative state for several breaths, absorbing the purity and brilliance of your Soul Star. When you feel ready, allow the light to gently descend through your entire body, anchoring divine insight and clarity in every cell. Gradually bring your awareness back to the present moment, carrying with you the serenity and guidance you received during this meditation.

Soul Purpose

Violet ~ Angelic Guidance

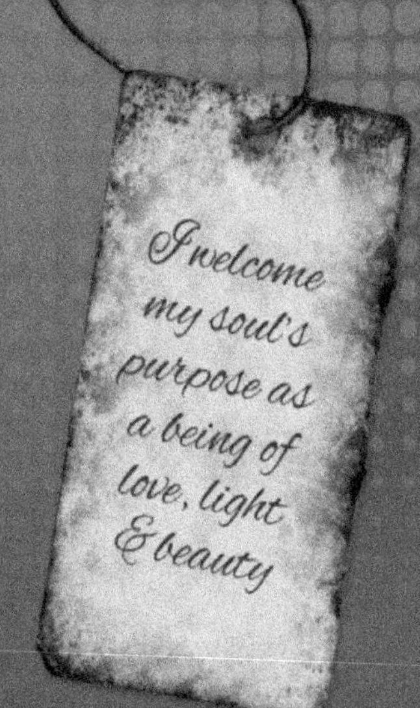

The ninth Chakra, or *God Portal Chakra*, is located about 12 inches above the head and is blue and violet utltra violet in color. This chakra is known to hold the Divine Template of your Soul's Journey which is in essence the keeper of your Spiritual Gifts. The Soul Purpose Chakra holds the information about your Akashic Records and it is also the chakra where we receive angelic guidance. When this center has awakened, you become a truly multi-dimensional being and your work will be to assist others in their awakening.

The function of this chakra is the access of information about Karma, lessons, our learning abilities, doorways to other dimensions and times, as well as the Akashic records. It is through this chakra that we view past life information. Occasionally we can obtain this information in the dream state, when there is important information to communicate to us. Often spirit/angels will use our dreams to get our attention. The dream state many times express ideas in symbols and it is our job to interpret the symbols presented. We can, of course, gain confirmation of our interpretation through meditation.

Soul Purpose Meditation

Turning within, take a moment to breath and listen to the whispers of your angelic guidance. Ask your angelic guidance a question about your life path, one that is important to you. Being very quiet, listen and wait for sensations in your body, especially your Solar Plexus center. The answer to your questions will often appear as sensations of deep peace, joy, excitement and vision that supports your life path. This is the way the angels communicate.

When this chakra is balanced there is a feeling of ease and grace. You feel like you have a angelic companion in life, guiding you through feelings of joy, peace and love throughout your day.

The only lasting beauty is the beauty of the heart.

Rumi

Destiny Chakra

Gold ~ Divine Service

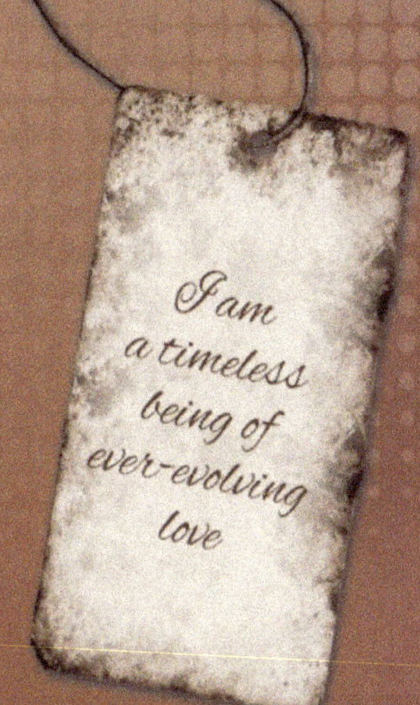

The Destiny Chakra, or *Grand Portal Chakra*, is located about 18 inches above the head and is gold in color. This is the chakra believed to be the pathway for soul travel into other parts of the universe including higher dimensions.

This is the chakra where true integration of polarities have occurred and you are now in complete equilibrium. When this chakra is completely open you are in a perpetual state of receiving high universal energy and have become a master whose life is dedicated to Divine service.

The Angelic Chakra contains the programming of the soul for this lifetime and the history of the soul. It is through our connection and understanding of this chakra that we gain (or affect) our own healings and insights. We also learn our lessons, understand the soul contracts and begin to understand our life purpose.

Destiny Meditation

I am open to the universes teaching. I simply ask "What am I to do" and "I allow life to bring me experiences and doorways to take me to my full potential. I affirm that my life is about Divine service and ask that all my actions be devoted to this purpose."

When this chakra is balanced there is a deep feeling of oneness with all of life. You walk the middle road, between the experiences of good and bad, pleasure and pain and you hold a deep peace within your heart that is not affected by outer circumstances.

Through love, thorns become roses.

Rumi

The Art of Meditation

Meditation is a state of communion with the divine – the pure essence of God within our heart. When the mind dissolves into the heart of stillness, it is possible to see the divine in all of creation. This gives space for the mind to be born anew and be purified from the past, leading ultimately to peace and freedom of being. Our true nature lives in each moment, is reborn in the next moment, and is constantly dying to the old. This renewal process of each moment requires us to practice letting go through our breath. With each inhale, we allow ourselves to become immersed in **What Is** the true vastness of being. With each exhale, we surrender our sense of separation. Through deep inner silence, we experience a unity in life, where all is laid to rest in the peace of the sacred force that is always present.

Five Steps to Meditating with Ease

1. Create a Sacred Space

Your meditating space should be free of clutter, electronics or distracting stimulus. You may want to bring a candle, crystals or other sacred objects to the space. Bring pillows and blankets so you can sit in comfort. Quiet spots in nature are also very conducive to meditation.

2. Find a Comfortable Seat

You can sit cross-legged in easy pose, lotus or hero's pose. You may want to sit on a pillow; this will assist in allowing your hip flexors to relax. Sit with a long spine and lower your shoulders away from your ears. You may want to sit against a wall to help your spine stay erect. Doing some light stretches prior to your meditation practice can help you sit with more comfort. See page,49 Daily Chakra Exercises, for some suggestions on exercises.

3. Set a Regular Time

Try to set a consistent time everyday for your meditation practice. The best times to meditate are at dawn or dusk, but it is more important that you set a time that works with your schedule. The more regular you can become with your practice, the easier meditation will come and the deeper you will go into silence. You will feel tremendous benefit in your body and mind from practicing meditation for just 10 minutes a day.

Hero's Pose

Come without memory or premonition.
Come blindly into it.
Sit without resistance.
Let your rampant vibrancy exchange with
the abstract and incomprehensible.
Feel the sweet death of being out of control.
There is no ending point.
Your surrender is the infinite language.
You are the co-creator of this uncommon
existence.
Dance within the rolling waves.
Fill the sky with your magenta dreams.
Put the world to bed under the
crystal night heaven.
The Fairy Tale is yours.

By Arya

4. Begin with Breath- Practice full yogic breathing in the beginning of your meditation practice. Inhale deeply for 3 seconds, allowing your belly to expand fully, and exhale for 3 seconds. With each exhale, visualize tension leaving your body and mind. Dedicate the first few minutes of your practice to intentional yogic breathing and then return to your natural state of breathing.

5. Become a Witness-

Close your eyes and retreat inward. Allow yourself to detach from your thoughts and impulses. Begin to observe the ebb and flow of your mind. Feel the fullness of your presence by just *Being*. Release anything that pulls you to move out of the stillness and spaciousness of the present moment. Your mind will still do as it always does, but as you retreat into the silence and fullness of your heart, you will find it easier to disengage from your thoughts and rediscover your own Sacred Presence.

Empty yourself of everything. Let the mind become still. The ten thousand things rise and fall while the self watches their return. The returning to the source is stillness, which is the way of nature.

Lao Tsu, Tao Te Ching

Begin at the Root Chakra

- Feel the vital energy of the earth as it enters the **Root Chakra**, intensely connecting you with the earth...

- Relax and allow your breath to assist in releasing tensions, worries and anxieties...

- Feel yourself letting go into a deeper and deeper state of peace...

- Breathe gently from your lower abdomen...

- Slowly, deeply, your breath moves throughout your being assisting you in relaxation...

- Let your awareness move to your lower abdomen, the base of the spine where the seat of the Root Chakra and the Kundalini reside. This is your grounding center, the foundation of your being...

- Feel a sense of belonging, inner security and trust, knowing that you are on a grand journey of life to the kingdom of your own divinity...

- Your purpose here is to trust, accept and learn the art of being. You have inner security and gratitude for the opportunity this birth brings...

- Visualize a glowing red sun here, nurturing and awakening your vital force within...

- Feel grounded and centered, let go of any insecurity within the sacred life force.

Move up to the Navel

- As your breathing comes into rhythm with the vital energy running up your spine, feel your awareness move to the sacral center, the center of cleansing water that circulates around your abdominal area, cleansing, refreshing and purifying physical and emotional toxins.

- Bring a golden-orange ray of vital energy here, allow your physical creative force to surface, embrace your passion for life and feel the miracle of the vital force within you.

Move up to the Solar Plexus

- As you move from the watery, creative substance of the second chakra into the fiery nature of the Solar Plexus Chakra, you feel alive with the flowing, vital current of your being. Embrace your sense of self and feel secure in life's process. Now allow your awareness to enter the fiery solar plexus region, the physical sun of your universe. This is the source of personal power, the chakra of transformation.

- As you move your awareness from personal identification to your true nature of the impersonal self, feel the glowing energy here. The golden color of the Solar Plexus center warms your entire being.

- Your breath takes you into deeper relaxation and ease as you allow any worries or concerns to be dissolved by the fire of the Solar Plexus, bringing a deep sense of peace and abundance.

Know that through the breath you can relax and bring calmness and healing light to all thoughts and emotions.
You are in the center of your radiance.
Allow the personal self to transcend its own sense of power to the power of divine will.
This requires a surrender of identification held in separation.
Know that you are one unified whole in union with the divine nature of your being.

Move up to the Heart

- Move from the flaming sea of the Solar Plexus to the gentle harmlessness of the **Heart** center, sensing your integration with light. There is a beautiful color of rose pink here representing unconditional love and a hue of green representing the healing light of the soul.

- You feel the love and compassion deep within your heart.

Move up to the Throat

- Bring this awareness of your true nature as you enter the Throat Chakra. The miracle of this center is knowing and expressing your truth so that all things beautiful and true in your life are manifested.

- Feel a light blue radiance here, as you open to the unlimited expansion of perception and divine creativity.

- Allow yourself to discern the truth, express the truth and listen within to the infinite space and unbounded consciousness of your divine essence.

Move up to the Third Eye

- The radiance of this center opens you to deeper levels of truth and you move into the **Third Eye - Ajna** center, the eye of wisdom and stillness, where you access unlimited perception and understanding of life.

- This wisdom center, bathed in indigo light, takes you to the infinite creation.

- You feel receptive and at peace with all of life as you penetrate the stillness of empty space.

- Thoughts dissipate in this stillness as you connect with the sacred force.

Your heart knows the way; run in that direction.

Rumi

- The journey has taken you into the realm of cosmic knowledge, beyond all concepts and thoughts.
- This silence carries you to the home of your true self; you now go into the integration force of the **Crown Chakra.**
- A brilliant purple light floods down through all your chakras, integrating and bringing their energies into balance.
- You feel unleashed from all the chains of temporary manifestation; you have moved into the eternal, free-flowing energy of the unbounded consciousness of the **Crown Chakra.**

Color Healing, The Aura and Chakras

The aura and chakra energies work together to create and maintain life.
There are seven colors that correspond to the seven chakras.

Root Chakra
Red: Base chakra, relates to passion, life energy, sexuality and creativity. Stimulated with Green, Indigo and Violet. Soothed by Red, Orange, Yellow and Blue. Red – Life, physical self, physical plane. Energizes vitality, creativity, power and courage. Stimulates nerves.

Navel Chakra
Orange: Sacral (adrenals), relates to physical movement, etheric health, well-being and joy. Stimulated by Red. Calmed by Blue, Yellow. Orange – Health, vital self, physical plane. Healing, wisdom, circulates prana, strengthens etheric.

Solar Plexus Chakra
Yellow: Solar Plexus (nervous system), center of recognition and self-worth. Stimulated by Red, Orange, Yellow, Violet. Calmed by Blue and Indigo. Yellow – Wisdom, emotional plane, power self, self-awakening, inspiring, stimulating, wisdom, digestive process, increases intellect and power of reason.

Heart Chakra
Green: Heart, relates to love, harmony and balance. Stimulated by Red, Orange, Indigo and Violet. Soothed by Yellow, Green and Blue. Green – Energy, healing self, mental plane, whole self, harmony, balance, stimulates heart, releases tension, and negative energies.

Throat Chakra
Blue: Throat, thyroid, relates to creative expression through sound, communication and truth. Stimulated by Red. Calmed by Blue, Indigo, Green and Yellow. Blue – Inspiration, peaceful self, mental plane, healing self. Truth, perfection, devotion, creativity, peace, calming, intuition, connects us with higher mental body.

Third Eye Chakra
Violet: Third Eye (pituitary gland), relates to creative visualization. Gathers instruction from higher self. Indigo – Intuition, inspired self, buddhic plane. Devotion, clarity, expansion of consciousness, cools, strengthens thyroid and parathyroid. Purifies blood stream, heals emotional plane.

Crown Chakra
Magenta: Crown (pineal gland), relates to the eternal, spiritual self, connects us to cosmic consciousness. Violet – Spiritual power, spiritual self, logic plane. Meditation, inspiration. Purifies blood, stops the growth of tumors.

We are born of love: love is our mother.

Rumi

Daily Chakra Care

Chakra Clearing Techniques

Begin the process of clearing your chakras by holding your palm chakras just above each chakra point on your body. Move your hands slowly in a counterclockwise direction over each chakra. This motion helps remove stagnant energy and clear away any harmful buildup. After you complete the counterclockwise movement, flick your hands away from your body to release the energy you have collected.

Once you have finished clearing each chakra, pass your hand over the area again, this time moving in a clockwise direction. Make at least one more clockwise motion than counterclockwise, ensuring the energy is rebalanced and revitalized. The number of clearing movements can be adjusted according to your intuition—pay attention to how each chakra feels and continue the motions until you sense that the area is clear.

Note on Chakra Transformation

Note: The chakras are tools for transformation. We balance them through a simple clearing motion (as described above), use them to understand our issues, and map our healing course.

Daily Chakra Meditation Practice

Daily chakra meditation involves gently centering yourself each morning and bringing awareness to each chakra, one by one. Begin by settling into stillness and grounding yourself in the present moment. As you become calm, visualize energy flowing freely throughout your body, starting at your root chakra and gradually rising to your crown chakra.

As you move your attention upward through each energy center, take a slow, mindful breath and invite clarity and balance into your system. If you notice any areas of tension or energetic blockage, allow them to release naturally, giving gentle, loving focus to any sensations or emotions that come forward. Let your intuition guide you to linger where you feel most drawn, trusting your inner wisdom to reveal where extra care is needed. Continue this practice until you sense all your chakras are harmonized and balanced, leaving you feeling refreshed, grounded, and fully aligned for the day ahead.

With each breath, invite clarity and balance into your system. Allow any blockages or tension you sense to release naturally. As you direct your focus to each energy center, notice any sensations or emotions that arise. Give gentle, loving attention to areas that feel heavy or stagnant, allowing your intuition to guide you. Linger where you feel most drawn, trusting that your inner wisdom will reveal where care is needed.

Conclude your meditation by visualizing all your chakras harmonized and balanced. This leaves you feeling refreshed, grounded, and aligned for the day ahead.

Kinesiology Guidelines for Chakra Testing

Preparation and Permission

Before conducting a chakra test using Kinesiology, carefully review the Kinesiology testing guidelines. Ensure you feel confident in your ability to perform the test accurately. Always obtain permission from your   client or friend before beginning any energy testing procedure. To begin, position your hand over or just above the chakra you wish to test; direct contact with the body is not necessary.

Testing Procedure

Begin the testing process by placing one hand over the chakra being evaluated and using the other to perform the Kinesiology test. Start with the Crown Chakra and ask the question, *"Is the Crown Chakra balanced?"* Observe the response:

- If the answer is Yes (balanced), the arm will remain strong.
- If the answer is No (unbalanced), the arm will become weak.

Repeat this procedure for each chakra, systematically assessing their energetic balance.

Chakra Locations and Attributes

- **Crown:** Located at the baby's soft spot. Associated with Integration, openness, and connection.
- **Third Eye:** Situated between the eyebrows. Linked to perception and proper understanding.
- **Throat:** Found at the throat area. Govern the expression of truth and responsibility.
- **Heart:** Located between the breastbones. Represents self-love and integration of mind and emotions.
- **Solar Plexus:** Just below the rib cage in the abdomen above the navel. Associated with emotional nature and integration of personal power.
- **Navel:** Located below the belly button. Pertains to relationships and self-expression in the world.
- **Root:** Found at the pubic bone, with the hand held above the pubic area. Relates to security, groundedness, and trust in life's process.

You have within you more love than you could ever understand.

Rumi

Energy Evaluation Using the Pendulum

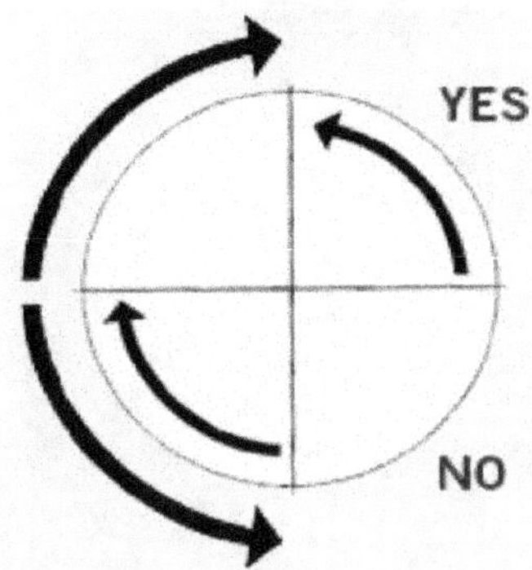

Pendulum Use for Chakra Evaluation

You may prefer to use a pendulum for energy testing rather than muscle testing. One advantage of this method is that you can perform it without the use of your client's arm.

Steps for Evaluating Chakra Energy with a Pendulum

1. When working with the chakras and a pendulum, place the pendulum over or in front of the chakra and observe the way it spins.

2. If the pendulum does not spin, the chakra may be inactive or under-energized. If it turns clockwise, this suggests the energy is unbalanced. A clockwise spin typically indicates the chakra is functioning well. You may notice differences in spin speed across chakras; those spinning more rapidly might require balancing. Often, breathing techniques and affirmations can help bring a particular chakra back into balance.

3. You can also assess the condition of a chakra by holding the
   pendulum over your palm chakra and, in turn, asking about
   each chakra.

Move up to the Crown

- The journey has taken you into the realm of cosmic knowledge, beyond all concepts and thoughts.
- This silence carries you to the home of your true self; you now go into the integration force of the **Crown Chakra**.
- A brilliant purple light floods down through all your chakras, integrating and bringing their energies into balance.
- You feel unleashed from all the chains of temporary manifestation; you have moved into the eternal, free-flowing energy of the unbounded consciousness of the **Crown Chakra**.

Color Healing, The Aura and Chakras

The aura and chakra energies work together to create and maintain life.
There are seven colors that correspond to the seven chakras.

Root Chakra

Red: Base chakra, relates to passion, life energy, sexuality and creativity. Stimulated with Green, Indigo and Violet. Soothed by Red, Orange, Yellow and Blue. Red – Life, physical self, physical plane. Energizes vitality, creativity, power and courage. Stimulates nerves.

Navel Chakra

Orange: Sacral (adrenals), relates to physical movement, etheric health, well-being and joy. Stimulated by Red. Calmed by Blue, Yellow. Orange – Health, vital self, physical plane. Healing, wisdom, circulates prana, strengthens etheric.

Solar Plexus Chakra

Yellow: Solar Plexus (nervous system), center of recognition and self-worth. Stimulated by Red, Orange, Yellow, Violet. Calmed by Blue and Indigo. Yellow – Wisdom, emotional plane, power self, self-awakening, inspiring, stimulating, wisdom, digestive process, increases intellect and power of reason.

Heart Chakra

Green: Heart, relates to love, harmony and balance. Stimulated by Red, Orange, Indigo and Violet. Soothed by Yellow, Green and Blue. Green – Energy, healing self, mental plane, whole self, harmony, balance, stimulates heart, releases tension, and negative energies.

Throat Chakra

Blue: Throat, thyroid, relates to creative expression through sound, communication and truth. Stimulated by Red. Calmed by Blue, Indigo, Green and Yellow. Blue – Inspiration, peaceful self, mental plane, healing self. Truth, perfection, devotion, creativity, peace, calming, intuition, connects us with higher mental body.

Third Eye Chakra

Violet: Third Eye (pituitary gland), relates to creative visualization. Gathers instruction from higher self. Indigo – Intuition, inspired self, buddhic plane. Devotion, clarity, expansion of consciousness, cools, strengthens thyroid and parathyroid. Purifies blood stream, heals emotional plane.

Crown Chakra

Magenta: Crown (pineal gland), relates to the eternal, spiritual self, connects us to cosmic consciousness. Violet – Spiritual power, spiritual self, logic plane. Meditation, inspiration. Purifies blood, stops the growth of tumors.

Would you become a pilgrim on the road of love? The first condition
is that you make yourself humble as dust and ashes.

Rumi

Angelic Healing for the Chakras

Preparing for Angelic Chakra Healing

Begin by taking a moment to relax your body and mind. Focus on deep, intentional breaths and gently release any worries, concerns, or stresses you may be carrying. This meditation invites you to invite the presence of Angels, welcoming their healing, balancing energy, and renewed vitality into your chakras.

Guided Visualization: Angelic Light Healing for the Chakras

Crown Chakra

Begin by envisioning a brilliant, angelic white light entering through the top of your head, gently passing through the Crown Chakra, often called the baby's soft spot. This chakra serves as your direct link to the Divine, always open to spiritual wisdom that guides your life's journey. Invite the angels to help keep this center clear of confusion, so you can maintain a strong connection to Divine guidance.

Third Eye Chakra

Allow the spiritual light to flow gently down your face, bringing soothing and healing energy. As the light moves through the **Third Eye Chakra**, located between your eyebrows, it empowers you to see your life from a spiritual perspective and supports inner vision, clarity, and truth.

Throat Chakra

The angelic light then descends to your Throat Chakra, where you gain the ability to recognize and speak your truth. Known as the Chakra of Miracles, this center gives power to your spoken words—ask the angels to express your authentic self and to voice your desires to the universe. Offer gratitude for all you have received, and observe the positive changes taking place in your life.

Heart Chakra

As the angelic white light continues its journey, it reaches your Heart Chakra, the center of unconditional love and the path of the Christ. Invite the angels to help heal any unresolved issues or misunderstandings related to love. Remind yourself that Divine love is unconditional and offers self-forgiveness. Your Heart Chakra is your sacred inner temple—a space to rest, reconnect with Spirit, and rediscover your true nature.

Solar Plexus Chakra

Let the angelic light enter your Solar Plexus Chakra, the center of energy and personal power. This is where you experience your earthly journey most deeply. Invite your angelic guides to help you surrender and relax at the Solar Plexus, and notice how peace and well-being begin to grow within you.

Navel Chakra

Next, invite the angelic white light to enter your Navel Chakra, the source of life, creation, desire, and passion. Invite the angels to heal and balance your desires and sexual energy, aligning them with your highest good. Affirm your self-acceptance and release any shame or feelings of abandonment held within this center.

Root Chakra

Finally, visualize the angelic white light flowing into your Root Chakra, the foundation of your being. Take a moment to remember your unique life purpose, knowing you are eternally safe and secure. Ask for divine guidance in discovering your true purpose, and trust that genuine security is found in Spirit. Release any lingering fear and recognize the gifts of divine creation within you.

1. The Root Chakra

The Root Chakra reflects the condition of several vital areas of the body, including the lower back, spine, kidneys, adrenals, reproductive organs, small intestine, bladder, and legs. Imbalances in this chakra may manifest as physical symptoms in these regions.

- Low back pain, varicose veins, hemorrhoids, and digestive disorders
- Sciatica, constipation, anemia/blood disorders, and allergic reactions
- Osteoporosis, pain in legs and feet, and stress-induced ailments

2. The Navel Chakra

The Navel Chakra is the source of energy and vitality. Signs of distress related to this chakra may appear in the kidneys, adrenals, sexuality, and sense of self.

- Ulcers, stomach pain, anorexia, and digestive tract disorders
- Heartburn, backache, and nervous disorders
- Jaundice, obesity, and problems with the liver, spleen, or gallbladder

3. The Solar Plexus Chakra

The Solar Plexus Chakra is closely connected to the digestive process, the assimilation of food, and emotional well-being. Stress in this area may cause tightness due to issues related to personal power and emotional sensitivity.

- Menstrual pains, kidney stones, urinary infections, and kidney problems
- Cysts, prostate problems, lower back pain, and testicular ailments
- Impotence, hip joint pain, weak bladder, and inflamed ovaries

4. The Heart Chakra

Imbalances in the Heart Chakra can manifest as heart weakness, life-force blocks, circulation problems, and general immune-system difficulties. Emotional challenges may also present as difficulty loving oneself or difficulty giving and receiving love.

- Coronary illness, asthma, backache, and rheumatism in the arms/hands
- Angina, allergies, shoulder pain, and skin problems
- Colds or lung infections, high cholesterol, and high/low blood pressure

5. The Throat Chakra

The Throat Chakra influences the metabolic system, the neck, the thyroid and parathyroid glands, and breathing. It also relates to emotional issues involving communication and the ability to listen and hear.

- Throat pain, speech defects, shoulder/neck pain, and vertebral pain
- Tonsillitis, dental problems, thyroid problems, and stuttering

6. The Third Eye Chakra

Imbalances in the Third Eye Chakra often relate to sight, the nervous system, and emotional issues surrounding perception and understanding.

- Migraine/headaches, conjunctivitis, sinus problems, and brain disorders
- Neurological disorders, schizophrenia, middle ear problems, and learning disabilities

7. The Crown Chakra

The Crown Chakra affects the entire body and may show signs of imbalance during severe illness. Emotionally, the

Crown Chakra relates to integrating life experiences on all levels.

- Headaches, paralysis, cancer, and mental confusion
- Immune weakness, depression, sleep disorders, and multiple sclerosis

Aromatherapy Through Chakra Fragrances

Aromatherapy is a gentle healing technique that harmonizes the senses and helps dissolve blockages in the chakras.

Root	*Cloves, Cedar, Jasmine, Rose, Patchouli, Myrrh, Musk*
Navel	*Ylang Ylang, Sandalwood, Jasmine, Rose*
Solar Plexus	*Peppermint, Lemon, Rosemary, Carnation, Lavender, Cinnamon, Marigold, Chamomile, Thyme, Juniper, Vertiver*
Heart	*Attar of Roses, Bergamot, Clary Sage, Geranium, Melissa*
Throat	*Sage, Eucalyptus, Frankincense, Lavender, Sandalwood, Chamomile*
Third Eye	*Rosemary, Juniper*
Crown	*Sandalwood, Jasmine, Rose, Lavender, Frankincense*

Use the earth's energies to balance the chakras or simple visualizations that use nature.

Root Center:
Lotus position sitting on earth. Any connection with the earth will balance the root as well as assist you in grounding your energies.

Navel Center:
Ocean, waterfalls, streams, lakes, ponds and all watery aspects of nature.

Solar Plexus Center:
Sun, fire, desert, heat, all warming aspects of nature.

Heart Center:
Connect with all green aspects of nature.

Throat Center:
Healing through connection with all blue aspects of nature, such as water, skies, etc.

Third Eye Center:
Healing through stargazing and night skies.

Crown Center:
Healing through climbing to high places, mountains.

 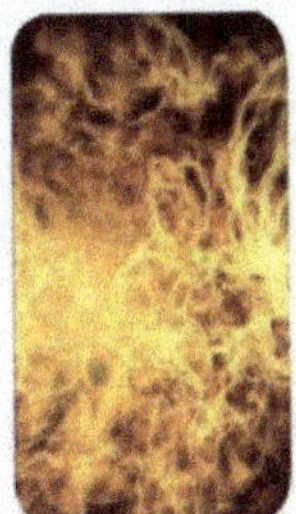 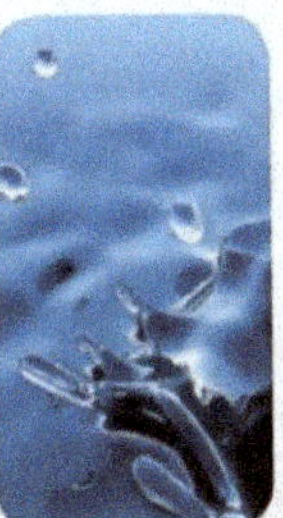 

Balancing the Chakras Through Nature

White Light Energy Protection, Clearing & Grounding

Whenever you feel energetically out of balance, drained, disturbed, negative or depressed, you might consider energy clearing to clear, balance and renew your energy.

Here are some tips to create a strong energy field.

- Use the light to create a force field of protection around your body.
- Create a shield of white light from your inner energy field, filtering all thought, feelings and emotions that are not of the highest good.
- Visualize a force field of white light surrounding and protecting your body. For protection, imagine a mirror around the body. This mirror reflects on the outside pushing away anything from us as if it is reflecting back to the source.
- Using white candles and incense, create a sacred space for your daily energy practice, take time to meditate, breathe and align your energy with your source.
- To ground and center your energy, imagine a silver cord through your spine, connecting you deep with mother earth.

To clear the aura, imagine you are under a beautiful blue waterfall. Allow the water to flow through your Crown Chakra, through your inner energy field and off your feet, clearing all unwanted accumulated energy.

Be certain that in the religion of Love,there
are no believers and unbelievers. LOVE
embraces all.

Rumi

Aromas are pure fragrances for healing body, mind and spirit. You can use the aromas in the form of incense, flower essences, and essential oils, or soaps, candles, and sachets. Aromatherapy is used externally and most are diluted with a base oil or carrier oil. Some of the carrier oils that can be chosen are sesame, coconut, sunflower, canola, mustard, sweet almond, avocado, calendula, carrot, hazelnut, jojoba, olive, peanut and wheat germ.

How to Use Essential Oils

Oils can be applied to chakras, alarm points, and emotional stress points and the point at the base of the neck called the release point. They can also be applied to points on the feet, such as K1, and to many points on the hand. Apply to the hand and rotate clockwise to activate.

Bathing:

Using oils in the bath helps unlock congested pores, eases muscle tension and fatigue, quiets the mind and calms the spirit. After running a warm bath, add eight to ten drops of your chosen oil and relax in the bath for at least ten minutes. **Suggested bath oils:** Bergamot, Chamomile, Frankincense, Geranium, Jasmine, Lavender, Mandarin, Neroli, Tangerine, Rose, Ylang Ylang. Add vegetable or olive oil for dry skin.

Bath Therapy: Put seven drops from a flower essence or essential oil bottle in the bath water. For best results soak for 30 minutes. Water is a conductor for electrical force. It activates the aura, cleanses the energy fields and releases karmic patterns.

Vaporization/Inhalation:

Inhale the essential oil by putting six to seven drops onto a tissue or cotton ball; take deep breaths for maximum benefit.

Massage:

Choose specific oils to suit the condition and temperament for the massage. Add ten to twelve drops to one ounce of massage oil. **Inhaled as a vapor:** Use two to three drops. Put hot water into a bowl, add the oil, cover your head with a towel, lean over bowl and inhale. Breathe in deeply.

Diffusers: Use candles or electric diffusers. Diffusers should be made of clay or glass.

Humidifiers: Add one to nine drops to the water.

Room Sprays: Four or more drops, per one cup of water.

Anointing:

Use Myrrh, Frankincense, Jasmine, Rose or Lavender on the Third Eye along with stating your affirmation or intention out loud. For protection use Rosemary, Juniper and Vertiver. Put on Solar Plexus and move the energy with a counter-clockwise motion. It is wonderful to use specific oils on the chakras, or on any area of the body that needs attention.

The Bach Flowers for The Chakras

ROOT: Sweet Chestnut – *Trusting yourself*

NAVEL: Wild Rose – *Taking part in life joyfully & fully*

SOLAR PLEXUS: Larch –*Self-awareness*

HEART: Heather – *Unconditional love*

THROAT: Wild Oat – *Communicating from your deepest soul*

THIRD EYE: White chestnut – *Aid to meditation*

CROWN: Olive – *Trusting in cosmic harmony*

Once all other chakras are in balance, the Crown Chakra is also balanced.

Let yourself be silently drawn by the strange pull of what you really love. It will not lead you astray.

Rumi

Symptoms: How to use Essential Oils

Aches & pains
Massage & Bathing: Lavender, Myrrh, Cinnamon
Inhalation: Basil, Sandalwood

Antibacterial
Massage & Bathing: Jasmine, Sandalwood, Myrrh
Inhalation: Gardenia

Congestion
Inhalation: Eucalyptus, Sage, Basil, Mint

Depression
Massage & Bathing: Lime, Basil, Jasmine, Thyme
Inhalation: Rosemary, Bergamot, Orange, Patchouli, Saffron, Ylang Ylang, Sandalwood

Digestion
Inhalation: Cardamom, Cloves, Marjoram, Lavender

Fatigue
Massage & Bathing: Basil, Cloves, Marjoram
Inhalation: Lavender

Gynecological
Massage & Bathing: Rose, Lemon, Rosemary
Inhalation: Geranium

Infections
Massage & Bathing: Eucalyptus, Cedar

Immune functions
Massage & Bathing: Myrrh, Frankincense, Rose
Inhalation: Lotus

Insomnia
Massage & Bathing: Marjoram, Lavender, Ylang
Inhalation: Chamomile, Sandalwood

Stress, Tension
Massage & Bathing: Rose, Lavender, Sandalwood
Inhalation: Neroli, Frankincense, Geranium, Clary Sage, Basil, Lotus, Lily

---

Essential Oils for:

Over-thinking & Worry: Sandalwood, Lemon, Frankincense, Myrrh

Depression & Fear Nervous:
Tension: Chamomile, Orange, Bergamot

Disempowerment & Indecision: Ginger, Juniper

Clarity of Mind: Rosemary

Anger & Frustration: Orange, Bergamot, Grapefruit, Peppermint, Chamomile, Yarrow, Lavender, Oil of Rose

Impatience & Intolerance: Bergamot, Lavender, Peppermint

Mental Fatigue: Rosemary, Tea Tree, Laurel

Tension & Agitation: Chamomile, Sweet Orange, Bergamot

Relaxation & Rejuvenation: Frankincense, Lemon, Peppermint

Anxiety & Apprehension: Basil, Bergamot, Clary Sage, Frankincense, Geranium, Grapefruit, Jasmine, Juniper, Lavender, Neroli, Orange, Patchouli, Rose, Sandalwood, Vanilla, Verbena, Vertiver, Ylang Ylang, Thyme

Bitterness: Chamomile, Bergamot

Nerves: Angelica, Basil, Bergamot, Camphor, Cypress, Jasmine, Lavender, Melissa, Neroli, Patchouli, Chamomile, Rose, Rosewood, Sandalwood, Tangerine, Vertiver, Ylang Ylang

Lack of Confidence & Self-Esteem: Rosemary, Jasmine, Rose

Low Morale: Thyme, Pine, Cedarwood

Lack of Self-worth: Rose, Jasmine

Anxiety & Depression: Lavender, Rose

Sudden Fear: Geranium, Vertiver, Rose

Calming: Jasmine, Ylang Ylang

Vulnerability: Pine, Thyme

Resistance to Change: Cypress, Juniper

Chronic Indecisiveness: Clary Sage, Bergamot, Orange

Frustration & Negativity: Bergamot, Orange, Neroli

Lonely & Forlorn: Marjoram, Rosemary, Myrrh

Over-attachment: Frankincense, Myrrh

Joylessness: Jasmine, Ylang Ylang, Orange

Abandonment: Rose, Neroli, Ginger

Depression: Basil, Bergamot, Camphor, Chamomile, Clary Sage, Geranium, Grapefruit, Jasmine, Lavender, Neroli, Patchouli, Rose, Sandalwood, Ylang Ylang

Nervous Tension: Chamomile, Orange, Bergamot, Lavender

Psychic cleanser: Rosemary

Spiritual protection: Rosewood, Sandalwood

The way the universe opens up to the heart that
loves-no pen can describe.

Rumi

The Healing Power of Crystals & Gemstones

Amber

Azurite

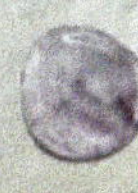
Amethyst

Alexandrite

Agate

Aquamarine

Aventurine

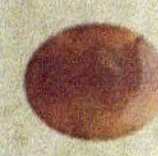
Carnelion

Chalcedony

Citrine

Celestite

Coral

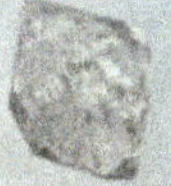
Diamond

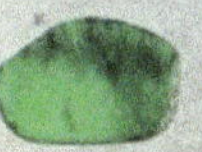
Emerald

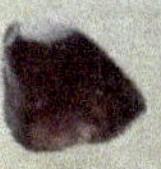
Garnet

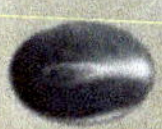
Hematite

Jade

Red Jasper

Kunzinite

Heart Kunzinite

Lipus Lazuli

Malachite

Moonstone

Crystals and gemstones have been used for thousands of years for correcting disorders in the physical body and energy fields. In the past, many valuable stones were crushed and reduced to ashes to produce medicines which were ingested orally. Gems may be kept in water, so that the water absorbs their vibration, and are then used as liquid remedies. The healing energy of gems is the energy of white light with specific healing properties. Crystals bring more beauty and light and change the energy of an area. Light reflected off a crystal brings healing and greater harmony. Crystals bring messages of great wisdom as well as energy that heals and transforms.

They have the power to receive, contain, project, emanate and reflect vibrations. Through using crystals it is possible to awaken one's dormant energies and to remove energy blocks. They also help align the energy fields with the greater universal energy fields. Through this alignment our energy fields are raised to a much higher level and we then develop intuition and a deep connection with the source of life. Crystals are mirrors of our soul and can be powerful tools on our transformation path, reflecting our true nature and our soul's gifts. Crystals, the most highly evolved in the mineral kingdom, are symbols of radiant white light energy. All crystals are expressions of light and energy and each has their own rate of vibration.

How Crystals are used:

- As remedies
- Worn as a talisman
- For pendulums
- For laying on of stones
- For meditation
- Can be held or worn to absorb properties
- Can be placed in visual range to aid in focusing
- For aura cleansing and balancing
- In jewelry as an aid in maintaining mental clarity, improving concentration and emotional stability.
- Used to clear away emotional debris and to enhance healing abilities.

Care and Cleaning

Place crystals where they can reflect their light and radiate their beauty. Cleanse new stones by soaking in sea salt water for at least three hours.

Recharging

Keep in a well-lighted room.

How to make Crystal Remedies

Place stones or crystals in pure leaded glass; fill with distilled water. Place in the morning sun for about three hours. The water will be infused with the vibration of the crystal as well as the color of the stone. Put in dropper bottles and test regarding the amount to take, or use approximately 10 drops several times a day. Work with the healing affirmations the stones represent. *See list of suggested affirmations along with meanings of stones.*

Suggested Stones for Remedies

Clear quartz, tourmaline, rose, adventurine and amethyst. Stones can also be used with creams or massage oil to enhance the effect of the massage. Green stones produce a healing affect, red and orange stones a revitalization affect, pink enhances love and heart opening, blue is calming and violet intensifies the connection with higher consciousness.

Programming Crystals

Thoughts, wishes and blessings can be programmed into crystals. Simply direct the affirmation or thought into a clear quartz crystal and the crystal will carry the message for you. Crystals will carry out whatever healing intention you might have.

I died from the mineral and became a plant
I died from the plant and became an animal.
I died from the animal and became a man.
Then why fear death?

Rumi

Gems & Balancing the Seven Primary Chakras

Opal

The seven chakras or centers of vital energy receive and transmit energy in the form of color. Their correct functioning depends on both psychological and health. Gemstone therapy has a direct action on balancing these subtle energy centers.

Onyx

The Crown Chakra rules the pineal gland, brain and right eye, and is balanced by Emerald, Amethyst, Fire Agate, Labradorite or Malachite and especially Diamond.

The Third Eye Chakra rules the pituitary gland, left eye, ears, nose and nervous system and is balanced by Topaz, Amethyst, Carnelian, Emerald, Labradorite, Malachite, and Sapphire.

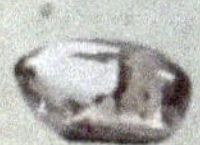
Quartz

The Throat Chakra rules the thyroid gland, bronchial and vocal organs, lungs, alimentary canal, and comes into balance through the Diamond, Amber, Aquamarine, Citrine, Emerald, Lapis Lazuli, Topaz or Turquoise.

The Heart Chakra rules the thymus gland, heart, blood, vagus nerve, and circulatory system and is balanced by Sapphire, Bloodstone and Topaz.

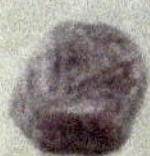
Ruby

The Solar Plexus Chakra rules the pancreas gland, stomach, liver, nervous system, and gall bladder and comes into balance with Ruby, Amber, Aquamarine, Citrine, Emerald, Moonstone, Pearl and Turquoise.

The Navel Chakra rules the reproductive system and comes into balance by the use of Pearl, Amber, Amethyst, Aquamarine, Carnelian, Coral, Fire Agate, Garnet, and Labradorite.

Rose Quartz

The Root Chakra rules the adrenals, spinal column, and kidneys and comes into balance through Coral, Garnet, and Turquoise.

Selenite

To balance the Chakras with the use of crystals or gems, first detect the center that needs balancing (see energy diagnosis page 39) then, when the person is laying down in a relaxed state, apply the stones to the center. (see chakra chart on page 38). Test for length of time. Music and quiet environment are important.

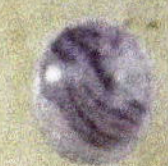
Sodalite

Healing with Gemstones

Sapphire

1. **Root Chakra** – Agate, hematite, blood jasper, garnet, ruby, bloodstone, smoky quartz, onyx, tiger eye.

2. **Navel Chakra** – Carnelian, moonstone, citrine, topaz, coral, tourmaline.

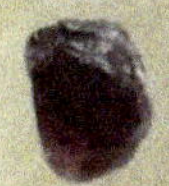
Tourmaline

3. **Solar Plexus Chakra** – Citrine, turquoise, lapis, amber, tiger eye, topaz, aventurine, quartz.

4. **Heart Chakra** – Rose Quartz, tourmaline, kunzite, emerald, jade, watermelon tourmaline, azurite, aventurine, quartz, malachite, moonstone.

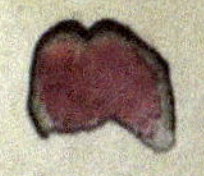
Tourmaline Watermelon

5. **Throat Chakra** – Aquamarine, turquoise, chalcedony, lapis lazuli, agate, celestite, sodalite, sapphire.

Topaz

6. **Third Eye Chakra** – Lapis, blue sapphire, sodalite, quartz, opal.

7. **Crown Chakra** – Amethyst, clear quartz, diamond, crystal, topaz, alexanderite, sapphire, selenite.

Tiger's Eye

Turquoise

**What? Are you still pretending you are
separate from the Beloved?**

Rumi

Daily Chakra Balancing Exercises

Chakra Clearing Exercise

This exercise is a powerful way to cleanse and rejuvenate all of your chakras. The lymph nodes under the armpits are rejuvenated by the vigorous motion of the arms in this exercise. Repeat this exercise whenever you need to bring instant clarity to your mind and energize your body.

1. Sit in a comfortable, easy pose or lotus pose. Root down through your tailbone and elongate your spine. Lift the crown of your head to the ceiling and allow your shoulders to lower away from your ears.

2. Interlace your hands into the Venus Mudra (lock), also known as the Mudra of Love. (Shown to the right) 

3. Lift your hands and elbows to your eyebrows, (the Third Eye Chakra). Keep your elbows in line with your hands and inhale fully.

4. Forcefully exhale as you push your hands and arms down until you reach your Navel Chakra (located three finger widths beneath your belly button).

Draw your stomach in-and-up at the end of your exhale. Lift your hands on the inhale and repeat this sequence 20-30 times vigorously. Let the inhale become automatic while the exhale stays powerful and forceful. Your eyes may be open or closed during the exercise.

5. Release the Venus Mudra. Close your eyes and with your palms facing your forehead, bring your hands toward the Third Eye Chakra. Return to full yoga breathing; inhale 3 seconds, exhale 3 seconds, until your breath returns to normal.

6. Move your hands from your Third Eye Chakra up to your Crown Chakra. Circle your hands down to the floor and bring your hands up to each chakra; starting at the Root and ending at the Crown. Visualize a white light rejuvenating each chakra center. Repeat these circles 3 times. Continue full yoga breathing.

Chakra Integration – Mother Earth & Father Sky

1. Begin by deeply inhaling and exhaling. Take a moment to focus your energy on your Crown Chakra.

2. Breathe in the energy from above your Crown Chakra and descend the breath down through the chakras, taking a full inhale and exhale at each chakra. Visualize the colors of each chakra as breath through them, and bathe them in a radiant healing light.

   - Crown - White or violet
   - Third Eye - Indigo
   - Throat - Blue
   - Heart - Green
   - Solar Plexus - Yellow
   - Navel - Orange
   - Root - Red

3. Now, with a deep inhalation, bring your arms out to your side.

4. Exhale and bring your hands together in front of your chest in prayer position.

5. Inhale once more and separate your arms away from each other, stretching one high above your head with your hands flat above the sky as if you were pushing the sky open – while the other arm reaches down flat as if you were pushing something downward toward Mother Earth. Gaze up at the heavens, (Father Sky). Stay in this position for 3 deep breaths.

6. Now, exhale as you return your hands to the prayer position, in front of your heart.

7. Repeat. This time switch your arms so the opposite arm rises to the sky while the other one pushes toward the earth.

8. Repeat up to 3 times for maximum benefit.

To love is human. To feel pain is human. Yet to
still love despite the pain is pure angel.

Rumi

Daily Chakra Balancing Exercises

Chakra Illuminating Exercise: Yogi Spinal Twist

The Yogi Spinal Twist is a powerful exercise designed to harmonize the right and left hemispheres of the brain, strengthen the lower back, rejuvenate the digestive system, and enhance flexibility in both the hips and the torso. This practice also aims to stimulate and awaken Kundalini Shakti, guiding her energy upward through the Sushumna channel to illuminate each chakra along the spine.

Step-by-Step Instructions

1. Begin your practice by sitting comfortably in a position such as Easy Pose or Lotus Pose. Focus on grounding yourself by pressing your tailbone into the floor, then lengthen your spine and gently lift the crown of your head toward the ceiling. Allow your shoulders to relax and drop away from your ears, releasing any tension you may be holding.

2. Place your hands on your shoulders, with your fingers resting in front and your thumbs at the back. Keep your elbows lifted and aligned with your shoulders, but keep your shoulders relaxed. Engage your core by gently drawing your belly button in and up toward your spine.

3. Inhale deeply through your nose as you twist your torso to the left, letting your gaze follow the movement. As you exhale, twist your torso to the right, allowing your eyes to follow the direction of the twist.

4. Continue twisting your torso from side to side, gradually increasing speed as you move. As you settle into the rhythm, close your eyes and visualize energy rising from your Root Chakra at the base of your spine, moving upward through each chakra along your spine, and finally ascending through your Crown Chakra at the top of your head.

5. Maintain this exercise for one minute. When you finish,
    slowly return to the center, place your hands on your knees
    with your palms facing upward, and bring your focus to your
    Third Eye Chakra. Visualize a vibrant indigo light shining
    between your eyebrows.

Balancing Your Chakras
Through Yoga!

The Sun Salutation also Balances all the Chakras

Jaya Sarada is a dedicated co-owner of Luminous Soul Center.

Jaya Sarada

Master Energy Healer and Educator

Jaya Sarada has devoted her life to helping others heal and experience spiritual growth. She serves as a channel for Divine Healing Light, supporting individuals through intuitive services and guidance to restore well-being. Jaya believes true healing is possible and shares her experience with those seeking assistance.

Credentials

Certified in Meridian Therapy, Kinesiology, Bio-Field Tuning, Reiki, Sound Healing, Vibrational Medicine, Akashic Healing and Soul Reading, Integrated Energy Therapy, Ordained Pathways of Light Minister, Transformational Counseling, Spiritual Response

Arielle Beaudy is a dedicated co-owner and practitioner of Luminous Soul Center

Arielle Beaudy applies her expertise in body mechanics, movement, energy healing, and holistic wellness to guide clients toward alignment and well-being. She integrates fascial release, trigger point therapy, and energy and sound healing to address pain and balance the energy field during sessions. Arielle also co-authored "Awaken Your Chakras: A Magical Journey of Transformation through the Chakras" with Jaya Sarada.

Credentials:

Bachelor of Fine Arts, Certified Sound Healer, Certified Yoga Teacher (Sivananda 1999 and Vinyasa Flow 2012), Reiki 1, Certified in Integrated Energy Therapy Level 1, Continuing Education in Restorative, Yin Yoga and Stretch Therapy, Holistic Nutritional Coach, Minister

Our Beloved Non-Profits

Luminous Soul – Center for Well-Being
Nonprofit 501(c)(3)

Our nonprofit is dedicated to promoting the well-being of women and children in our community—caring for body, mind, and spirit. We offer transformational healing sessions and educational programs, both in person and online, focused on energy and sound healing. Our services include yoga classes, mentoring, certification pathways, mental and emotional health support groups, and uplifting community events. Each offering is designed to enhance overall health and joy.

With more than 30 years of experience in the healing arts, our classes and services are deeply rooted in practical knowledge and sustained practice. This foundation enables us to deliver innovative, life-changing approaches to healing. We believe that every individual possesses a unique, innate ability to heal, which can be nurtured through regular self-care and supportive well-being practices.

We are committed to guiding individuals through their journeys of spiritual awakening, self-healing, and inner transformation.

Awaken Your Light

Through a blend of ancient wisdom and modern healing modalities, Divine Light Foundation and Luminous Soul Center for Well Being offers healings, teachings, and experiences to support your soul's evolution. Whether you are seeking energy healing, spiritual guidance, or a deeper connection with your divine essence, our intention is to illuminate your path.

Our Energy-Based Healing Modalities

Our healing modalities are designed to create a sacred space for personal transformation, spiritual renewal, and inner peace.

For those unable to attend in person, Divine Light Foundation offers remote healing sessions that provide the same benefits as in-person treatments.

Benefits of Our Healing Modalities

Emotional Release & Healing

Our healing practices support the release of deep emotional blockages, freeing you from burdens such as fear, guilt, resentment, and unresolved trauma. By clearing these emotional patterns, you can experience greater emotional freedom, inner peace, and resilience.

Physical & Mental Well-being

Through relaxation techniques and stress-reduction practices, our modalities help reduce anxiety and tension. These approaches foster overall vitality, support mental clarity, and encourage balanced physical health, contributing to a sense of wholeness and well-being.

Spiritual Growth & Awakening

Our offerings awaken your intuition, deepen your spiritual connection, and help you align with your soul's purpose. As you nurture your inner wisdom, you become more attuned to your spiritual path and experience transformative personal growth.

Energetic Balance & Alignment

By restoring harmony to your energy field, our modalities help you achieve clarity, peace, and a sense of inner strength. Balanced energy supports both emotional and physical well-being, laying a foundation for lasting transformation.

Healing Past Life & Ancestral Patterns

Our approaches help clear karmic imprints and inherited energetic patterns that may hinder your personal growth. By addressing these influences, you can move forward with greater freedom and embrace new possibilities for your life's journey.

Contact & Additional Information

To learn more about our offerings and services, we invite you to explore our websites:

www.divinelightfloundation and www.luminoussoulcenter.com.

For questions or to connect with us directly, please email jaya@divinelightfoundation.org or love@luminoussoulcenter.com.

You may also reach us by phone at our toll-free number: 1-855-505-3935.

Heartfelt Closing

With much love and blessings, we extend our deepest gratitude for your presence on this journey. May your path be illuminated with joy, clarity, and spiritual fulfillment.

Sincerely,

Jaya and Arielle

www.ingramcontent.com/pod-product-compliance
Lightning Source LLC
Chambersburg PA
CBHW061036050726
47592CB00004B/1465